TELL HIM

Bob Duncan

ISBN: 978-1-950088-96-6

Dedication

To my wife, who lived most of this with me; and is still with me after 58 years of marriage. To my children, who were young and only heard small bits and pieces of the story. To my grandchildren, that live in a new era, and we shelter and protect as much as possible. To my friends who still like me with all my faults.

Acknowledgment

Thanks to Dot and Bert Crowley, coach Nelson and everyone that helped on this journey of life.

About the Author

A person born into difficult times that tries to live by the mottos:

"WHEN THE GOING GETS TOUGH, THE TOUGH GET GOING"

"NEVER GIVE UP"

Pat,
I hope you enjoy the book. It took 60 years to get the courage to finish it.
We met you + Dick before the trial which was after we moved from Gladwin.
I LOVE YOU
Bob

Prologue

Steps echoed mutely as she walked hesitantly down the antiseptic hall of the hospital's emergency room waiting area. She stopped before the young boy sitting alone on the bare oak bench. His emergence into manhood was suggested by the nearly invisible dark shadow on his upper lip. His normally bright gray eyes were dimmed by the tears that filled them to near overflowing.

He looked up into the compassionate face of the middle-aged nurse. She sat beside him, gently taking his hand into hers and said, *"I am sorry, Robert, but your father just passed away."*

The boy just stared into space. Tears began to run down his cheeks like a swollen stream escaping the confines of its bank and onto his clean, well-worn shirt.

"But you don't understand!" he said almost too loudly. *"I never got to tell him that I loved him!"* Following this proclamation, he broke into high, heavy sobs. He clung tightly to the woman sitting beside him.

It was senseless. His father was murdered, shot to death in front of his wife and within earshot of his son. It was neither a crime of passion nor of greed. It was an insane act of random selection, one for which an explanation could never be uncovered and one for which the boy would be tormented for the rest of his life.

His life was not easy. Struggling to avoid gang membership, being brought up in an environment of mental instability, living in poverty, and being labeled white trash by his peers; he was making a difficult transition into manhood to discover all too late that it was not a sign of weakness to tell one's father that you loved him; a discovery that would only add to his torment.

A discovery he can only hope other people will not have to make.

Contents

Dedication .... *i*
Acknowledgment .... *ii*
About the Author .... *iii*
Prologue .... *iv*

Chapter 1- Early Life *1*
Chapter 2- The Unfortunate Turn of Events *29*
Chapter 3- Life Moves On! *43*
Chapter 4- Life as a Quarterback *56*
Chapter 5- College Life *74*
Chapter 6- Trial *92*

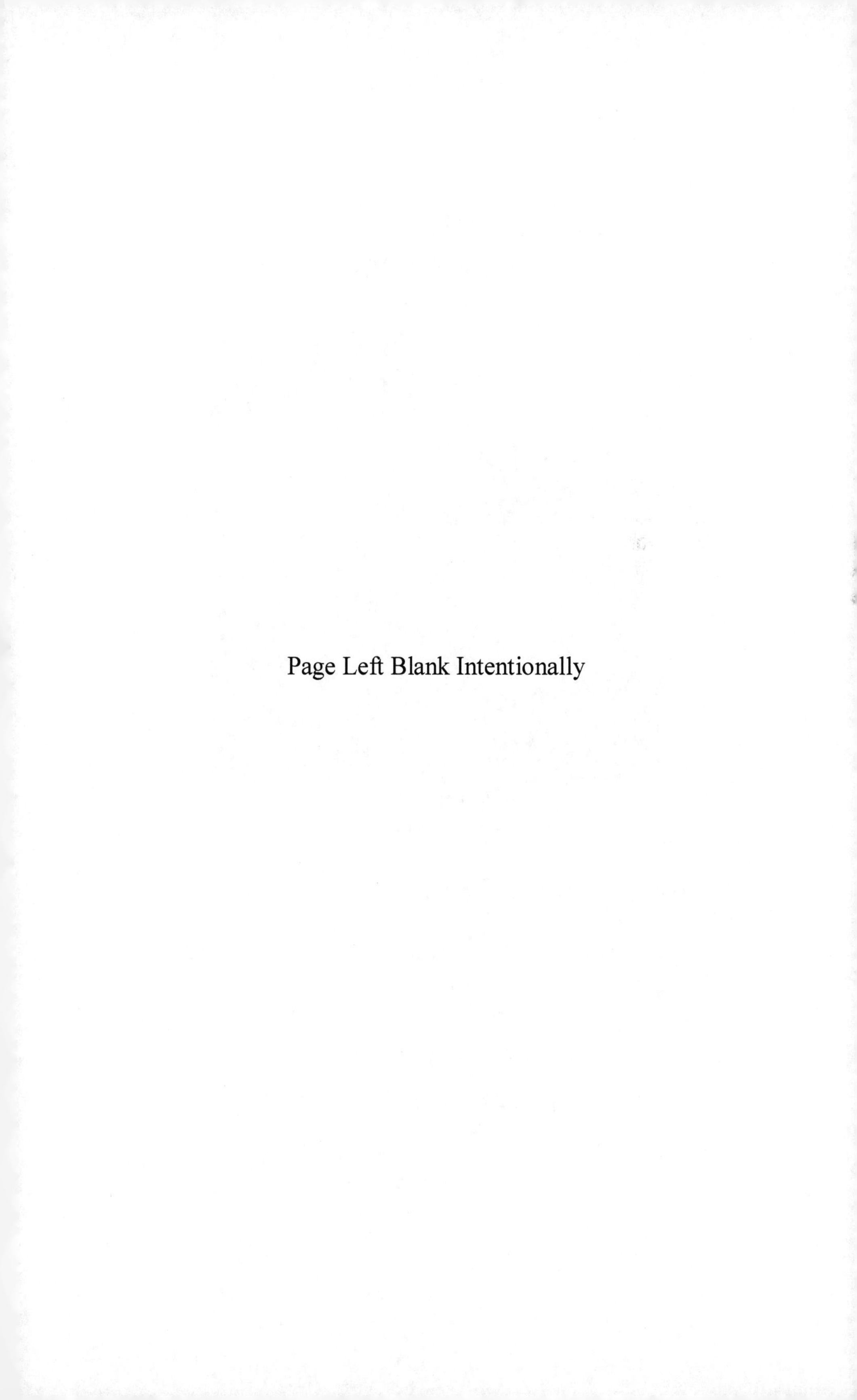

Page Left Blank Intentionally

Chapter 1
Early Life

Bob, Viola, Chris
Dog – Ranger

Detroit, MICHIGAN 1941

"*God, it hurts!*" The pregnant woman screamed as her shrill voice echoed throughout the house.

"*Just a little push honey, breathe!*" exclaimed the worried husband seeing his wife in agony.

"*Here it comes!*" Dr. Godard assured and let out a sigh of relief after having his ears done in by the screams he had been enduring for the past few minutes.

Dr. Godard smiled, "*It's a boy, Congratulations!*" The woman had pushed for the final time and out came the little boy in the hands of the doctor.

The whole room lit up with joy.

And so entered the world little Robert Eugene Duncan, aka, Bobby Gene Duncan. A skinny little boy whose life would be filled with adversity, violence, and pain and yet he never would stop chasing after success.

This day, marked the beginning of the story of Bob. Who was born during World War 2 in 1941, in the suburbs of Detroit, Michigan, Bob came into this huge world but in a very small house.

He didn't know that, but he had been born in a community consisting of poorly educated adults that worked in factories and gas stations, doing small businesses and manual labor to get by each day. When the Duncan's had moved to Michigan from Indiana, they had bought a small residential lot in the subdivision on

Hazel Street for $50. Initially, they had lived in a tent with no electricity or water. Bob had missed out on some of the worst days that his parents and his half-brother Ralph had to live with when they had first arrived here. They didn't even have proper means for ensuring safe sanitation. They had to dig a hole and build an outhouse just to go to the bathroom. They had to endure a very primitive living in those days. But that was how this community had started with people living in tents.

This was when Bob's parents met Dot and Bert Crowley. The Crowlies had moved from Mt. Pleasant, Michigan with three children so Bert could also work in a factory. Dot and the three children eventually moved back to Mt. Pleasant because of the primitive living conditions. Bert worked during the week and went to Mt. Pleasant on week-ends.

After a few years, Bob's father built a two-bedroom home on that same very lot. Two coal stoves heated the house. The county finally released electricity and water. The house had an inside bathroom by the time Bob had arrived in this world. The coal for heating the stoves was kept in a small shed behind the house, which was called a coal shed. The coal was delivered by a dump truck. It dumped the coal into the shed. Bob wasn't born when the Duncan's lived in tents; Bob was born in the house in his parent's bedroom delivered by Dr. Godard. The family couldn't afford to go to a hospital, so Bob was born in their newly built home. In the two-bedroom house, Bob lived with his mother, father, and Ralph. Ralph was Bob's stepbrother who was born out of his mother's first marriage.

His mother and father weren't educated individuals, his mother had only passed 5th grade, and his father had somehow scrambled through the 8th. Bob's father worked in a conservation camp in California after the depression before he came to Detroit. This was so that young men could work in government projects such as trimming forests and building schools.

A vast majority of the money Bob's dad made was sent home to feed his family. Bob's dad worked in the redwood forest in northern California. He did this to feed his mother, who was abandoned by his father and his three brothers and two sisters. His mother had two daughters and three brothers that lived in Indiana. When

Bob's dad returned from the conservation camps in California, he worked in agriculture at tomato canning plants that made ketchup, picked crops, and kept busy in the summer.

Bob's Uncle John, who was the only concerned brother of his father, moved to Detroit and obtained a job in an automobile factory here. He started insisting Bob's father and all of his friends to move to Detroit ever since he arrived there.

"*Get a job in this automobile factory and settle down here. Bring your family with you.*" He sat him down one day and spoke to him with sincerity and seriousness.

While nodding, Bob's father expressed his thoughts on the matter, "*I know you are right, but it's not that easy.*"

"*You need to try before you say that!*" exclaimed Uncle John.

Bob's dad, following that advice, got a job in an automobile factory, manning machines that made small engine parts for vehicles.

Years flew by, and soon Bob arrived to complete the small family of Duncan's'.

Bob's dad always worked the 3 to 11 shift because he got an extra 6 cents an hour for working that shift. This shift was difficult for the family because Bob only saw his dad on the weekends.

"*Honey, I am going to work.*" Bob's dad informed his mother as he walked to the door before Bob could catch up with him.

However, he failed to escape as Bob came running from his room calling out to him.

"*DAAAAAD!* "*When will you be back? You promised to help me with my geography project today instead of going to work. Then we were going to make dinner together.*" Bob asked innocently reminding him of all the plans that they had made last night.

"*I'll be back soon, my dear.*" Bob's dad left, giving a vague answer to him knowing very well that by the time he will be back, Bob would be fast asleep.

Bob and Ralph only had their mother to supervise them during the week. Their mother was not able to control both the boys together. She generally chose to let them listen to the radio instead of forcing them to do chores which she knew would only make her life difficult.

The boys would listen to programs such as Amos n Andy, inner sanctum and Friday night fights with Joe Lewis as the heavyweight champ.

"It's *finally Friday, and I can listen to the fights!*" Ralph planted himself on the couch as he turned the frequency of the radio to his liking.

"*NOOOOOO!!! Amos n Andy is on, and we are going to listen to that?!*" Bob screamed in protest.

But when he noticed Ralph wasn't changing the channel, Bob grabbed the radio and attempted to run, but Ralph's long arms snatched it out of his hands.

Bob was helpless in front of Ralph since Ralph was 9 ½ years older than him, so he sat down quietly to listen to whatever he got.

Ralph was rebellious and did not like school. In one instance, Bob remembers that when he was 5 years old, Ralph had been starting high school, and a school bus used to come to get him. One morning, he missed the bus intentionally.

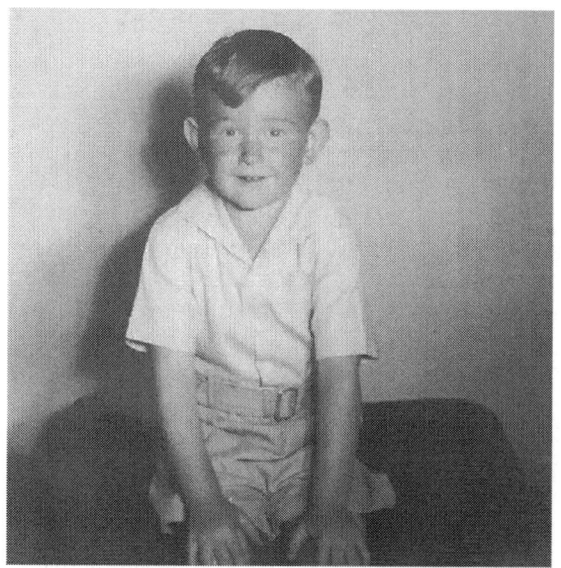

Bob at age 5 ready for school

"*Ralph, honey, are you feeling okay?*" Mother had asked him only to open the door and see Ralph alright and well, reading a comic book.

"*Get up this instant and get ready. I am dropping you off to school myself!*" Mother slammed the door and left, knowing that she had scared Ralph enough to force him to go to school. Although the mother knew that Ralph was becoming more and more disobedient by the day, she couldn't control him. She dropped him at school only to find him smoking by the grocery store in town two hours later. After that, she decided not to try and discipline him at all. However, the day Ralph turned 14 years old, their parents sent him away to live in Ohio with uncle Jigs, who was their mother's brother.

Uncle Jigs and his wife were famous for being very strict and stern. Uncle Jigs and his wife Gladys had two children. One was Norvita who was 12 years, and another was Dale who was 8 years old. Bob's parents had thought that Ralph would finally get disciplined at uncle Jigs' place.

"*Young man, you are in our house now, and you will abide by our rules!*" Jiggs scolded Ralph the day he had moved into their house. He had been told about all of his histories.

"*Sure I will,*" Ralph answered under his breath.

"*What was that?!" Uncle Jiggs asked him harshly glaring at him angrily with his beady eyes.*

"*Nothing,*" Ralph replied shortly and walked inside his room, slamming the door in his face.

Ralph was more difficult than what Jigs and Gladys had anticipated. So they sent him back to Michigan after a short stay. After coming back from Ohio, Ralph didn't go back to school. The schooling system in Michigan thought he was still in Ohio, and Bob's parents knew that due to this, Ralph would skip school every day. So, they decided not to send him to school and let him do whatever he wanted to. He wasn't much of a student anyway.

While Ralph was a handful, Bob was the child that his parents had always hoped for. He played with other kids in the neighborhood after coming home from school. He was tamed enough. He played hide n seek with other children along with kick the can, Cowboys and Indians, War with toy guns, Tag, Baseball, Football, and Basketball.

Bob enjoyed school and was an above-average student. In third grade the school wanted Bob to skip a grade. Bob failed the test on purpose because he did not want to be the smallest kid in the class. Bob was always average at all these games, but he enjoyed a lot playing with his friends, and he was blissfully away from all the worries in his life. After a while, the coal heaters in the house were replaced with a floor furnace with fuel oil as the fuel source. Bob's father built a two-car garage for one car. And a working shop on the side where the second car should be. He used it for woodworking, and he enjoyed it thoroughly.

The coal shack was no longer needed, and it was moved behind the garage into the alley. This shack became Bob's playhouse. When Bob was 6 years old, he had a friend named Billy. They always played together. They were floating small, flat pieces of wood with points on them and a hole drilled with a rod stuck in it in place for a sail.

From left to right
Dad (Gene)
Mom (Emma)
Grandpa Francis
Bob (age around 6)

Bob at 7 years of age with Ranger (dog)

They were floating them down the stream into the woody area. The whole neighborhood stayed out of the woods simply because it was not a safe place to be. As Bob and Billy raced their sailboats down, following them and running, both of the kids found themselves in the middle of the woods. As they looked to find a way out, they ran into some older kids. They began to pick on Bob and Billy, slapping them and threatening them. Billy and Bob both started crying. They told them to leave them alone.

Bob told them to stop and started yelling at them.

"*Stop, or else I will tell my brother!*" He made an empty threat.

"*Yeah, will you now? What's your name you monkey?!*" One of the big bullies pushed him mockingly into a nearby tree.

"*Bobby Gene Duncan!*" Bob replied, trying to shove the big boy away from him but failing miserably and falling backward.

"*STOP, or I **will** tell my brother!*" Bob threatened them again as they surrounded him and Billy one more time. Billy and Bob were both crying and scared.

One of them finally asked, "*Who is your brother, anyway?*"

"*Ralph Linley is my brother,*" Bob answered and saw a complete change in the situation.

The bullies froze. They couldn't believe what they had just heard. The little kid they were bullying was the younger brother of a gang leader. Of course, Bob didn't know that back then. The bullies begged Bob to not tell his brother, and they would never bother Bob ever again the bullies backed away from them and disappeared into the woods within minutes. However, Bob started looking up to Ralph as an all-powerful hero who had saved him in his dire need. He hoped that he could hold such power as well, someday. Shortly after that, Bob told his parents that he wanted boxing gloves and punching bags for his birthdays.

He even got himself, old army training manuals on hand to hand combat. Bob studied them and learned hip throws, shoulder throws, arms locks, leg locks, and pressure points. He figured out vulnerable areas for his defense. But Bob still relied on Ralph for backup against older kids. During springtime, when kids from elementary school would walk home, they would have to cross the woody area, and the bullies would always wait for the kids in that area.

They would stop the kids, take things from them, including their money, pens, and lunchboxes. If the kids didn't give them these items, the bullies would just beat them up and take their things from them anyway. Bob was never bothered by them because they knew that

Ralph was his brother, and they respected that. Although Bob would sometimes have to fight back a little bit, that was just until someone mentioned that Ralph was his brother. Bob became a leader against the bullies among children in his age group. Bob even thought of himself as junior Ralph. Parents in the neighborhood would not allow their kids to play with bob and his friends because of their bad reputation.

Bob and his friends would not leave any stone unturned for bullying the new kids who could come to reside in their society. It seemed Bob led the children in his group to become rebels at a very tender age. His brother Ralph led a gang of teenagers and young adult hoodlums. He continued to live at Bob's parent's house but came and went whenever he wanted. Bob's parents had no control over him, especially since Bob's father worked from 3-11 PM.

Ralph worked construction off the books because he was underage. He might've been 15 when he was working and doing man's work. Ralph didn't converse a lot with Bob, but Bob still looked up to him and idolized him. Ralph led a gang of about 20-40 young men and wore leather jackets and rode big motorcycles even before the hells' angels were a thing! Ralph always carried a hand-made blackjack with him which was a lead pipe, three and a half inches long and a rope loop which would go around his wrist so that it always stayed attached to him. It was wrapped in a black electrical cloth tape so that no fingerprints would be imprinted on it. He would use it to break the facial bones of people who would not comply with his orders.

"*Hun, Jacob, and Andy just got sentenced to life for murder*," said Bob's dad to his wife.

"What? Those are Ralph's friends! Bob's mother replied with distress.

"*Yes, don't worry. It's not our Ralph.*" Bob's dad comforted his mother.

"*I know, but he is the king of those idiots, it's not long before he is arrested too!*" His mother said sighing sadly.

Bob overheard them and that day. He realized that these were really bad people and his brother was their leader. Bob's crew would sometimes go to the end of the street and hang out outside the grocery store drinking coke and smoking cigarettes. Sometimes, they would steal something from the grocery store to eat, like candy bars and different things. Ralph became attracted to a 15-year-old girl named Viola when he turned 20 years old. Before they knew it, Ralph had gotten her pregnant. Ralph was forced to marry Viola because his only other option was to go to jail for rape because Viola was a minor and he was 20. This didn't stop Ralph from leading his gang, though.

Ralph and Viola rented a small house across the alley about two houses away from Bob's parents' house. They had a big yard which was large enough for their two boys, Chris, and Rodney to play. Viola became pregnant for their third child shortly after their second boy Rodney was born.

One evening at approximately 8:30 PM as Bob and his mother were sitting in the lounge area of their house. They heard quick but delicate knocks on their back door. Bob's mother got up to see who had decided to visit them at this hour. It couldn't be her husband. He didn't get off of work until 11. And even if he was here, why would he knock so gently? So Bob's mother started moving towards the door. Bob followed her closely. Bob's mother opened the door, and Viola came in and leaned against the wall. Viola was eight months pregnant and from head to toe covered in blood.

"It's Ralph, he went crazy and started beating me," said Viola crying hysterically.

"Come here, child. Sit down." Bob's mother hugged Viola, sat her down, and got her water.

"All I said to him was that he couldn't afford going out with his gang, and he went crazy," Viola said as she cried even harder.

That night, Bob started hating his brother, the one he had looked up to all his life. Bob thought that no one should do that to anyone, let alone a woman. Bob made a promise to himself that day that he will not turn out like his brother.

Bob's mother helped Viola in every way she could, whether it was with the kids or just hearing her out, Bob's mother was always there for her. Shortly after this debacle, Ralph was arrested and sentenced to probation. Viola's dad, Mr. Rose, became very angry over the fact that Ralph did not get jail time instead was just put on probation. The judge explained the situation and his decision of putting Ralph on probation instead of giving him jail time. Putting Ralph in jail will put the cost on the county of keeping him there. Then an additional cost of welfare that will go towards Viola and her two kids with the third one on the way this will only increase the cost to the county.

All of this was the reason that the judge gave Ralph probation instead of jail time so he could keep working.

Mr. Rose tried to get Ralph in an altercation at a local store where Ralph and his gang hung out. After Mr. Rose antagonized Ralph one of the gang members told him,

"*Ralph will not touch you. But someone else might prevent you from getting home on the three-block walk if you don't leave this instant and never come back*".

Mr. Rose made a quick and wise decision and left immediately without saying anything. Bob was told all of this by one of Ralph's gang members, and this only made his doubts about Ralph concrete. The promise he had made to himself of not ending up like Ralph seemed a good decision. Bob started hating Ralph and kept thinking that only an animal could beat up a pregnant woman or anyone else as viciously as Ralph did.

Shortly after the Viola incident, a new kid moved into the block named Sammy. He wanted to lead Bob's gang.

"You either fight me, or you join me!" shouted Bob at Sammy.

"I'll fight you, right here!" Sammy replied, smugly.

Sammy was a year or two older than Bob, but the fight for leadership was still scheduled. They fought. They took turns punching each other. Sometimes, Sammy would connect with a punch and then sometimes Bob would connect. Bob tackled Sammy to the ground and got on top of him and controlled him there for a bit until Sammy took advantage of his age and took control of the fight.

Exhaustion settled in both of them, as they went on panting and bleeding. Both of their shirts got covered in mud because of the takedowns. The fight lasted for forty-five minutes or an hour. Sammy reigned victorious at the end of the fight, and there was a new leader in the neighborhood. Bob was not sad about it. He wanted to leave the gang life behind anyway. He did not follow Sammy, and in doing so, he was shunned by other kids since. Sammy would not allow them to converse with Bob. Bob wanted people to like him, not fear him. At the age of thirteen, Bob lost his hold on his gang completely. After being shunned, the resentment from his old friends who he had not treated well when he was the leader of the gang became a reality.

They knew that with Bob's training of hand to hand combat and his natural leadership aura, they would not be able to take him on in one on one combat. So these old friends started picking on him with groups of two or three. Facing all of this, Bob went to Sammy and told him that he was being harassed by a few of his gang members.

"Sammy, some of your "boys" have been harassing me, and I won't say anything to them, but I will gladly kick your ass again to get them back!" Bobby threatened him angrily and walked away. And it all stopped. Even though Sammy had won the fight he had with Bob when they had fought for leadership, Bob put up a good fight

and hurt Sammy immensely. Bob was not afraid of getting hurt or to bring hurt upon Sammy and Sammy knew that. The harassment stopped, but the shunning continued. Bob's nose would bleed every two or three days after the initial brawl he had with Sammy. Bob believed that Sammy had the same issue with his nose; that's why he was so scared to fight Bob again.

Forgetting his past, Bob started focusing on school and studies. Bob had been an above-average student since he would read Ralph's school books. He learned how to do long division in the 1st grade. He became friends with other good students who were more focused on studying than on other things like gangs. But the problem Bob had now was that all of these new friends lived several blocks away.

It was not always safe to travel through the Mexican neighborhoods, the black neighborhoods, the Irish neighborhoods, and other hostile neighborhoods. At the age of 13, everything started to fall apart for Bob. The automobile factory closed down, and thousands of men were unemployed, and Bob's father was one of them. Bob's dad had poor health, and with him being middle-aged, it was hard for him to find employment. Bob's dad was 6 feet 1 inch tall and weighed 112 pounds. The labor market was flooded because of the shutdown. Bob's mother got a job in a small factory for a short time before having a nervous breakdown, and she started staying home after that. This led Bob and his family to go on welfare. Bob started looking for a job and landed one delivering newspapers. He delivered them on his bicycle regardless if it was summer or winter, and he went delivering for seven days each week.

He managed to save up $600. His parents borrowed the $600 from him to use as a down payment on a small piece of land so that they could build a house on that piece of land. But due to the unavailability of money, his parents had to forgo the lot, and Bob had to say goodbye to his $600. His parents promised to pay him back, but the circumstances didn't allow for that to happen.

The people from the welfare department gave Bob a red sailboat for his birthday, and he was excited to sail it on water. It was spring, and the ditches in front of Bob's house had two or three-foot water in them. Perfect for his red sailboat, he put the boat on the water, and it tipped over. He tried again and again, but it kept tipping over and over again. After about fifteen unsuccessful tries to sail his boat, Bob went home. Later, someone pointed out that the sailboat was not complete. The keel needed to balance the weight of the boat was missing, making the boat top-heavy. Bob made another promise to himself that he would never be on welfare again. They had given him a broken sailboat.

At 15 years old, Bob entered high school. The name of his high school was Taylor high school. It was a large school that Bob rode the bus to get to. It was a tough school. Bob joined the cross country track team and practiced after school. He saw fights after school on a regular basis. But he went to this high school for only a little while before he went to California.

Bob ended up in California after Ralph had his fourth child and decided that the gang life was not good for his future. He moved to California with his wife to work. He then called Bob's parents to California since they were not able to find a job in Detroit. So Bob's parents sold the house they had built, packed up and went to California with Bob. Ralph worked in northern

California throughout the week and came home on the weekends. After moving to California, all of them lived in one house, all nine people. Bob went to high school in California, but that was short-lived because Bob's parents were still not able to find employment. Bob loved California because the weather was much better than the cold weather of Detroit, and he loved the ocean.

While Bob was enjoying California, it became tougher and tougher to find jobs for his parents. His parent's friends Bert and Dot Crowley used to live in the tent next to them. Bob's parents stayed in contact with them throughout even after they moved to California.

They informed his parents about a small grocery, gas station that had living quarters in the back that was available to rent on the highway M20, between Mount Pleasant where the Crowley's lived and Midland. Crowley's made a deal with the gas station people and Bob, and his parents drove back to Michigan. The Duncan family arrived in Michigan in April. The parents set up the store with inventory and gas. The living area was simple, and it came equipped with a kitchen, living room and two bedrooms; they were very comfortable here. Bob rode the school bus to Shepherd High school, which was 15 miles away. The Crowley's had a son named Carl who also went to Shepherd high school and he and Bob both were freshmen. Crowley's had two other children, Barbara was in the 8th grade, and Ron was in the 7th grade. Bob felt very fortunate to have a friend already in high school after attending two previous high schools with no friends.

Bob made it through tryouts for the junior varsity baseball team and got selected to the first nine for the team, and life was good. During this time, Bob experiences his first love. He saw a cute girl walking on the sidewalk of Shepherd high school and quickly became intrigued by her. Not knowing who she was, he moved on and went to practice.

As he was practicing with his team, he saw three girls sitting on the bleachers and watched them. The cute girl he had seen earlier was among those three girls. He kept looking at her, stealing glances just so he could steal a glance at her face again. The girl got up, and Bob saw her leaving, and as she was leaving, she ripped her skirt on a nail on the bleachers.

Bob dropped everything and went to see if he could help her, but her friends quickly hid her and took her off the field and into the back of the bleachers. Bob didn't know that this cute girl was going to be his future wife.

Soon, the business at the gas station was good, and Bob was getting odd jobs at the farms in the area.

He wanted to earn money as soon as possible to get independent quickly!

Chapter 2
The Unfortunate Turn of Events

Back side of store where Duncan family's car parked

Labor Day, September 2, 1956

Bob Duncan's life in Shepherd, Michigan brought new hopes and dreams for him. However, it also brought many disappointments and painful occasions. Things were going good in the Duncan household. Bob was finally happy after a long time. This was the beginning of his sophomore year at Shepherd High School.

He was expecting it to be as awesome as his freshmen year had been. He had been able to grab a few jobs here and there, and he had found a girl to drool over in his dreams. Things had never seemed so good to him, and he was only 15 years old!

Bob couldn't wait for school days now. He found his school just that amazing. The Labor Day weekend was just one more holiday that he would be spending away from school. After that, he would be able to meet new friends at school. He hoped this day would pass quickly. He had been expecting this weekend to be rather boring, but he had never imagined what happened on that day instead.

At about 7:30 AM, on the morning of Labor Day, Bob's entire life turned upside down. He had been sleeping in the second bedroom of their small living quarters at the back of their gas station and food store when he heard gunshots. Startled, his eyes flew open, and he shook himself out of bed. At first, he thought the loud bang had been from the blaring television. But he knew at the back of his mind. Only real gunshots could be that loud. He pulled on his pants over his trunks and rushed into the living room. The second his eyes fell on the floor before him, he froze. His father was lying on the floor, clutching his chest. There was blood all over the floor, and the lamp on the side table was knocked over.

"What happened?" Bob bent down to help his father, but his father shook his head as if telling him not to come too close.

*"A man... shot me... took your mother..."*His father answered. He could barely speak. His words were a near whisper.

Bob gulped down. Panic rose inside his chest as he stood torn between going after the kidnapper or staying with his dad. Finally, he asked the first thing he could think of, *"Where are the shotgun and the ammunition?"*

His father answered, *"The closet..."* His voice had turned even weaker than before.

Bob went to the closet and pulled out the shotgun. He checked the chambers for any shells. They were empty. He searched for the shells in the drawer, found them and began loading the gun. He had the shotgun loaded in a few seconds, and as he cocked it and made for the door, he heard his dad's weak voice from the floor once more. It stopped him dead in his tracks. His heart began racing faster than ever.

"Bob, call the police... and the Crowley's... be careful..."

Bob rushed to the phone and made the call. He looked out the windows to see if anyone was still lingering about. He had the shotgun in his hands, and he was careful of each step he took. He returned to the living room where his dad lay and knelt down beside him on the floor.

He had kept the barrel of his shotgun pointed at the doorway. He was ready to shoot if the bastard who had shot his dad tried breaking in again. No one came, and after several minutes which seemed like hours, the police and the ambulance arrived. All the while they waited, Bob's dad never made a sound, never moaned. It was as if he knew his pain would be unbearable for his son. He kept looking at his father every now and then to see if he was alright.

Bob was only 15 years old, he was not ready for any of this, but he was in this situation without a clue of what was going to happen the next second. He sat there as if frozen. He didn't even twitch a muscle while they waited. He wanted to do something to protect his father, but he didn't know exactly what he could do.

When the police and the ambulance arrived, they took Bob's father to the hospital. The police questioned Bob about what had happened. Bob didn't want to let his father go alone, but after reassurance from the medic that his father would be taken care of, he calmed down. Bob was still in shock. He couldn't think straight let alone answer questions.

He tried his best and repeated the few facts he had known about the shooting and his mother being taken by the shooter. He couldn't even define what he was feeling. He was on the verge of breaking into tears, and at the same time, his shoulders felt so heavy, he could barely stand on his two feet.

"Tell me, son, what happened," The policeman asked him in a calm and sweet voice.

"I don't know, I was asleep, and I woke up..." Bob tried to answer but started crying as he spoke up.

The policeman placed his arm around him, *"Be strong son, everything will be alright. We will catch that bastard. I need you to tell me everything you can recall."*

Bob nodded, sobbing, *"Is my dad going to be alright?"* He innocently asked.

"Yes, he will be." The policeman answered confidently.

Bob wiped the tears quickly and started telling the cops everything he knew about the shooting and kidnapping.

Bert Crowley arrived shortly after the police were done questioning Bob. The second Mr. Crowley saw Bob, he hugged him. Bob clung on to him tightly. Mr. Crowley asked the policemen where they had taken Bob's father. He took Bob to see his father at the hospital.

While Bob and Mr. Crowley made their way to the hospital, the police set up a roadblock at the highway to catch the perpetrator and rescue Bob's mother.

They caught the shooter at the roadblock.

The police brought Bob's mother to the hospital. Bert Crowley and Bob had arrived at the hospital by this time, and they sat down in the waiting area after confirming that Bob's father was in the emergency room. Mr. Crowley sat beside Bob and tried to console him. Bob was blankly staring ahead.

To him, there was no noise in the hospital, just mumbles. Bert would get up every few minutes to ask the doctor about Mr. Duncan. When there was no news for a while, he went to explore. When he was gone, a nurse approached Bob. Her steps echoed as she walked hesitantly down the anti-septic hall of the hospital's emergency room waiting area.

She stopped before the young boy sitting alone on the bare oak bench. She read the name on the slip she had received from the reception, Bob Duncan. She looked at the boy sitting almost bent double, his face in his hands. His entrance into manhood was visible by a light trace of hair on his upper lip. His normally bright grey eyes were dimmed because of the tears that had filled in them since he had arrived at the hospital.

He looked up at the nurse expectantly when he realized she was standing over him. The nurse sat beside him and gently took his hand into hers. She looked into his eyes and said, *"I am sorry my son, but your father just passed away."*

Bob just stared into space for a few seconds. Then the impact of what she had just said hit him, and he burst into tears. Before he could stop himself, he was crying his heart out. He exclaimed quite uncontrollably, *"I never got to tell him, I loved him..."*

Bob broke into heavy sobs. He couldn't control himself. He clung tightly to the nurse sitting beside him. He cried a river that day. He just couldn't stop. The nurse tried her best to console him. Mr. Crowley stepped in and held Bob tightly. He had just heard this bad news from someone at the reception desk. *"It's going to be okay, I promise, It will be all alright."*

Bob said nothing, just cried. He fell asleep in Mr. Crowley's arms. Bert laid him down on the sofa when the policemen came in to tell them that they had apprehended the assailant.

It was senseless the way Bob's father was murdered, shot to death in front of his wife and within earshot of his son. It was neither a crime of passion nor of greed. It was an insane act. One of random selection and one for which the explanation would never be uncovered. One for which Bob would be tormented for the rest of his life.

Bob's life had not been an easy one, struggling to avoid gang membership, brought up in mental instability, living in poverty, labeled as white trash by his peers and as he was making his transition into manhood he discovered all too late that it was not a sign of weakness to tell his father that he loved him. A discovery that would only add to his agony, one he hoped that other people would not have to make.

The police interrogated Bob's mother about the incident as her husband took his last breath. Bob's mother explained that someone knocked at the storefront door at 6:30 AM. She had felt odd at an early arrival. Regardless, she got out of bed because Mr. Duncan was a heavy sleeper and she didn't want to disturb him. She answered the door but didn't open it. She just informed the guest that the store was closed.

He begged for gas because he needed fuel to get to Midland. Bob's mother asked him to wait for a minute. She was still in her housecoat. She unlocked the gas pumps, unlocked the front door and went outside to pump the gas.

The morning was beautiful, and she was enjoying the weather as she pumped the gas, she even thought about going to the park after breakfast. She told the police officers that she didn't notice anything suspicious regarding the man. He had looked like an average Joe to her.

After she was done filling up the gas in his car, he quickly came up to her and stuck a gun in her ribs. *"Get in the car or else I am going to shoot you right here."*

Gasping and scared, Mrs. Duncan tried to fool him. She said, *"My husband is right in there! I am screaming if you don't let me go!"*

Graham, the assailant, laughed menacingly, *"Call him, I'll shoot him first."*

"Don't do anything, I am going, I am going" Bob's mother had replied out of fear.

Graham forced her into his car and drove towards Midland. As they were driving down the road, he told her that he had beaten up his girlfriend at Mount Pleasant and the police were probably looking for his car according to her description. He decided to change cars by returning to the store and taking the Duncan car. The police would not be looking for their car.

When Graham and Mrs. Duncan returned to the store, Bob's dad was awake and dressed. Mrs. Duncan entered the house, and Graham walked in behind her. She put up a finger on her lips to signal Bob's father to stay quiet.

They were all standing in the living room, and Mr. Duncan shouted, *"What the hell is going on?"*

Before he had taken a step toward the assailant, he had shot Mr. Duncan. He didn't stop at the first shot as the first bullet grazed his arm. He shot him the second time in the chest as Mr. Duncan fell to the floor, bleeding profusely. The assailant fired two more shots into Mr. Duncan's torso. He forced Mrs. Duncan to get the car keys, and they left. Mrs. Duncan ended her statement amid a flood of tears. She didn't know why all of this had happened to them, but she hoped that the maniac who had killed her husband would at least get the punishment he deserved for the crime he had committed. After a while, the Duncan family learned that Graham had been examined by three psychiatrists while he was in police custody. They declared that he was insane. He never went to trial due to the plea of insanity. He was sent to the Ionia State Hospital for the Mentally Insane with the condition that if he were discharged or recovered from his illness, he would be tried for his crimes.

Mr. Duncan's funeral was held in Indiana where he originally lived before moving to Michigan. The funeral was very sad and bleak. The death of Bob's father came as a shock to everyone. Mr. Duncan was only 43 years old with three brothers, two sisters and uncles, aunts, friends and many people in the small town of Indiana. He was loved by everyone.

He was a kind and gentle man who cared for his family and friends with all of his heart. He was a hard worker and did all he could to provide for his family emotionally, physically and financially. It was a very sad time that someone like him had departed from this world.

To Bobby, his mother and his dad's friends, it seemed like the world had ended with the death of Mr. Duncan. Everyone wanted to tell Emma; Mrs. Duncan, how sad they were. At the same time, they wanted to hear all the details of the abduction and murder. Bob felt like an abandoned child. No one consoled or approached him. He was sitting at a bench alone, left at the mercy of his thoughts. He began blaming himself for the whole thing.

Thoughts like *'...if only I was awake I would've stopped him, if I had gone out instead of mother, if I had woken up earlier then I would have been able to save my dad...'* messed with his head throughout the funeral. He never quite got rid of these thoughts later in his life. He didn't know that years later he would learn from Bert Crowley that there was nothing that the doctors could've done to save Mr. Duncan's life.

4 bullets had been fired into him, 2 of which were shot at him at point-blank range while he had laid on the floor. Everyone seemed to wallow in their own sorrow and never tried asking Bob about how he felt. When Bob and his mother returned to the store a week after the funeral, they restarted their life. Without Mr. Duncan, it was very

hard, especially when everything reminded them of him, but they understood that it was something they had to do. They had to move on.

Store where Bob's Dad was murdered

Fifteen year-old Bob and his Mom in the store after the shooting

Chapter 3
Life Moves On!

"The dead never truly die. They simply change form."

-Suzy Kassem

Days after his father's passing, Bob felt as if he was floating. He didn't know what was happening to him. He couldn't control anything. He had never known he would be spending his high school days without his father to guide him, but here he was, still breathing. Nevertheless, with Graham off the hook, there wasn't anything else that Bob could do to avenge his father.

He had no idea how he was going to get back at the man who had ruined their lives and yet he had to put aside his thoughts to move on in life. Though Bob's father was no more in this world, he was still alive in their memories. It was indeed quite difficult for Bob and his mother to live without a father and husband, yet they had to. There was not a single day when they didn't cry remembering him. They were trying very hard to be back to a normal life.

Every day, customers would come and inquire about Mr. Duncan. The news of his suspicious murder had spread all around. The painful and heartless questions from the customers about the ordeal would open their wounds. Bob's grandfather Mr. Gilligan moved in with them, tried to give them a male figure to look up to.

When Bob went back to the high school, the first day he met Carl Crowley, Carl suggested something that he had never expected.

"Hey, Bob! How are you? I hope things are better at your side," Carl asked empathically.

"I hope things can be better someday," Bob sighed. Carl could feel the pain in bob's voice.

"Well, Bob! I have something to tell you," said Carl

"What?" Bob asked in an unenthusiastic tone.

"You are going out this year for the high school football team." Carl was excited because he knew Bob loved playing football. Although he had only played outside of school, he was good at it.

"But I have never played organized football, and I don't know how to put the equipment on," Bob told Carl.

"Don't worry, dude! I will show you how to put it on" Carl patted Bob's shoulder.

Carl had a friend named Gary Hines. Carl took Bob to his friend. Gary sold Bob a pair of high top football shoes for $2.00. Those shoes were too big for Bob; however, he used those shoes for his entire high school football career.

Bob was delighted that he was going to be a part of the high school football team, yet he was nervous about how he would perform. Everyone in the team except Bob had already been practicing for a week. They had their gear. Bob got the leftover gear.

The pants were so huge that Bob had to wrap tape around the legs to prevent them from falling down. The shoulder pads were too small. He got an old cardboard helmet. There was not a single piece of equipment which was perfect for Bob. Mr. Nelson was the coach for their football team. He would coach junior varsity and varsity. Varsity football practice would take place at noon, and junior varsity practice was after school. Parents would pick junior varsity kids after they had gotten off work, and the kids had finished their practice. On the first day of practice, Carl told their coach Nelson that Bob had played football in his old days.

"Bob! Which position you have played the most?" Coach Nelson asked Bob.

"Well, you put me where you think I should be", answered Bob as he had never played any position except sandlot football.

Coach Nelson put Bob on defense as a linebacker because he was not the appropriate size to play on the line. Becoming a linebacker meant that offensive players would run over Bob on every play. Bob, however, was ready to take the challenge. He listened to his coach and practiced tackling properly.

Gradually the run overs were reduced as he had mastered tackling. Bob played as a linebacker in his first game for the freshman team. The following week he played as a middle line breaker for the junior varsity. Bob loved playing these games. His anger and anxiety would calm down when he would play in the field. Playing football was working as a stress reliever for Bob. He had never realized before that his intense anger prevailing inside his body was because of his father being murdered.

He played as a middle linebacker in the third game of the season also. Coach Nelson asked Bob to be a co-captain in the fourth game. It was the happiest moment of Bob's life. Bob would become a madman while tackling in the game. He told his defense *"The other team does not get over the 50-yard line into our territory."*

Once an offensive player was tackled on their 48-yard line.

"Not acceptable," Bob whispered in his heart and then grabbed the player's ankles and dragged him out of their territory.

Bob was yelling, swearing crazily all over the field. A referee came over to Bob and said, *"Young man, you are playing a great game, but if you do not stop swearing, I will have to kick you out of the game."* Bob, however, continued to play hard without his profanity. He didn't know if it was his luck or something else, but he just kept getting better at the game and a time came when he got a leading position on the junior varsity football team. The 5th week of the season Bob was promoted to varsity at middle linebacker. Varsity had different helmets, and all were being used by players.

Bob had a large head, and only one second-string offensive player wore the helmet that Bob needed to play. This player did not like Bob even though Bob only played defense. Bob didn't play in the first three quarters. Bob was ready to tell Coach Nelson he would rather play junior varsity than stand on the sideline of varsity game.

The fourth-quarter started, and Nelson asked Bob to replace middle linebacker on defense. Bob played the entire fourth quarter and was very happy. By the sixth week, he started and played the entire game. Sophomores didn't make the varsity. The Jr. and Sr. players started disliking Bob. They tried every dirty trick to make Bob look bad in practice. They never knew that their malicious tactics actually made him a better player. Bob closely watched their tricks, and it helped him understand where the play was going. Coach Nelson was more than a coach for Bob. He always guided him like a leader, friend, and an elder brother. He could see the spark in Bob to ace the game. Bob used Coach Nelson's valuable guidelines to play against juniors and seniors on their football team. Coach Nelson had instructed him

"There are always 2-3 offensive players that will lean towards the play, look at the person they will block when they come out of the huddle, wet their fingers when throwing or catching the ball, shoulders up when it is a pass and shoulders down for a run."

In the seventh and eighth week, Bob played every defensive play and had fun. The last game of the season they played Clare High School. Clare was undefeated until Shepherd spoiled their record by upsetting them and finished the season 6-2.

Bob intercepted a pass to stop Clare from scoring. Only four sophomores earned Varsity Letter that season. Bob was one of them. The other three were the back-up quarterback, Dave Dunham, back-up lineman, George Yost, and Art Carroll as a back-up running back. Varsity letter also called monogram is an award that is a major accomplishment for an athlete. Obtaining a Varsity Letter at the beginning of his football career was indeed proof of Bob’s capabilities.

He eventually became a quarterback, a journey which is quite unforgettable!

****

Bob’s mother was running the store, but the business was declining with each passing day. Meanwhile, Bob's mother, Emma, met a man named Louis. He had a good job at a factory in Midland. Emma married Louis. It was just a matter of time now until the store closed. Although things were changing for Bob, he felt, from here onwards they were only going to get better.

His belief kept him focused on his path to recovering from the loss of his father. In time, he grew fond of Louie. In the fall of Bob's junior year in high school, Louie and Emma would live in a one-bedroom trailer about 40 feet long and Bob would sleep on the kitchen table. He used that table as a bed because he had no other option. Life was very cramped in the trailer. Bob’s mother was tired of driving 12 miles every day to the Crowleys to pick him up at night. So he would usually spend the night in a spare bedroom in their farmhouse. Living with the Crowleys during his junior and senior years of high school made Bob's life easier. During his stay with Crowleys, Bob worked with Carl on different summer jobs. He would pull weeds, clean junk areas, and do anything to earn some money.

During these afterschool practices and games, Bob would commute with Carl because he had a driver's license and he was one year older than Bob. Crowley always had a lunch packed for bob in the morning. Crowley's were always there to support Bob and his family.

Those were the days when Bob came across that cute girl once again, the one he saw in the spring. Her name was Caroline. They were in the same typing class. Bob was extremely happy those days. He would keep staring at her during the entire class. Caroline was a friendly girl. She always had a great smile on her face. Bob would always develop a pleasant feeling in his heart when he would see Caroline. Seeing her would always bring a cheerful smile on his face. Bob didn't realize when he fell in love with her. The feeling of being in love with an amazing girl was indeed out of this world for Bob.

It was Bob's 16th birthday. Barbara Crowley had arranged a birthday party for Bob at their farmhouse. It was a surprise party for Bob. They invited Caroline also. When Caroline entered the farmhouse, Bob felt that everything was brightened all of a sudden.

"You're here!" exclaimed Bob. He was extremely happy. Caroline's presence made him believe that she cared for him. She presented him with a short-sleeved shirt with red patterns on it.

Bob & Caroline together

Bob had been through a lot of difficult phases in his life. Nevertheless, there was a naughty and mischievous kid inside him. During his sophomore year, Mrs. Stewart was his English teacher. She would drive a Ford Thunderbird convertible to school. She would always brag about everything.

Once she told the class, *"My eighth-grade students find my jokes were so funny. They almost fall out of their chairs, laughing."*

The mischievous child inside Bob woke up. He had never found any of Mrs. Stewarts jokes funny. He agreed with three or four boys in his row to fall out of their desks when Mrs. Stewart would tell a joke next time. In the next class, Mrs. Stewart started telling a joke, and Bob suddenly fell out his chair and laid on the floor.

Mrs. Steward was shocked. She had no idea what was going on with Bob on the floor. Bob was also embarrassed because his buddies did not fall on the floor.

"What is this, Bob?" Mrs. Stewart asked him.

Bob reminded her of her comments about her eighth-graders and said, *"I found your joke very funny. It caused me to fall out of my desk chair."*

Bob thought Mrs. Steward would get angry, but she laughed and said,

"Aww, Bob! That's really cute."

After that, she always had a smile for Bob even out of the class in the hallways.

Bob & Caroline at county fair 1958

Bob & Caroline at the Jr. Prom

Chapter 4
Life as a Quarterback

Bob is practicing quarterback prior to Edmore Game which was played in a blizzard.

Bob still wore his oversized shoes worth only about $2. He wasn't one to show off. Bob started at left cornerback at the beginning of the junior year because of his tackling ability and reasonable speed. George Yost became the middle linebacker. The Left defensive end that played in front of Bob was Art Carroll. Art was the best football player Bob ever played with.

Art was 185 pounds of muscle and VERY fast! The two of them were a great unit. Art stopped the run, and Bob stopped the pass. Art would tell Bob what he was going to do so they would not make a mistake. Bob saw him rush the quarterback and tackle him behind the line of scrimmage. He also saw him Art rush the quarterback, knock him down, chase the ball carrier behind the line of scrimmage, and tackle him for a loss. If he could not catch the ball carrier, Bob's job was to contain and slow him down so Art could tackle him from behind for loss.

Sometimes the ball carrier tried to run outside Bob that resulted in a large loss. If it looked like a pass, Art contained the corner and Bob covered the receiver. After a few games, their opponents seldom attacked their side. For the year rushing attempts they averaged minus (-3) yards and zero pass completions on their side of the field. One game against Harrison early in the season, the right tackle was trying to poke Art in the eyes.

Art told the player to stop playing dirty and even went to the referee to complain. The poking continued, and Art told Bob he was tired of the dirty play and to watch the next play because Art was going to make it stop.

Art came out of a three-point stance with a fist to the stomach of the opponent and raised him 2-3 inches off the ground! When the play was over the referee stopped play for the injured player and the Harrison player was carried off the field and never returned.

Another thing they would do when the other team stopped running or passing their way played out of position. Bob and Art always discussed their plans with each other to eliminate any confusion that might hurt the team. Sometimes Art would play very wide, leaving a large opening for the other team to run through. They would close that hole quickly if the opponents took the bait and ran their way.

Sometimes Bob would position himself 20-25 yards in a wrong area and wait for the opposing coach to notice and try a pass in the open area. They finally stopped this procedure because it drove Coach Nelson crazy.

The last game of the football season was coming up on Friday night. On Monday, Bob and his team were preparing for the final game. While they were scrimmaging, Dave Dunham who was the quarterback of the team fumbled the ball, and before the coach could blow the whistle, to stop the mad scramble, a group of players jumped on the ball and on each other without warning. Dave took the brunt of the incident in the worst possible way. He got severely injured and broke his leg. This unexpected incident four days before the last game shattered the entire team. Coach Nelson was immensely distressed. He called out Bob.

"Bob! I want you to be the quarterback on Friday night. Can you do it for the team and for me?" Coach Nelson asked bob in a troubled tone.

"Coach! I am a defensive cornerback. I have never played any offense. How can I be a Quarterback when the final game is just around the corner?" Bob was puzzled.

"Bob! I know you can do it!" Coach Nelson was determined to motivate Bob.

"But what about the second string Quarterback Coach?" Bob was still perplexed.

"I don't feel comfortable with the second-string quarterback to replace Dave; we do not have much time left, Bob. You need to practice for the next three and a

half days to play our quarterback. I am confident. You won't let us down!" Coach Nelson had already decided that only Bob would replace Dave.

Bob agreed to give it a try and practiced tirelessly for the next three and a half days.

Friday night was one of the most important nights of Bob's life. He had to prove his abilities. He had to make his coach proud. He was playing as a quarterback for the first time. It was Shepherd vs. Edmore High School.

The weather was a blizzard with winds blowing at the speed of 50 to 60 miles an hour. When the game started, the field was wet with one or two inches of snow on the ground. After the first half, the snow was three or four inches deep. The middle linebacker of the opponent team was an arrogant guy.

He tried to threaten Bob. Bob, however, used those threats to turn the game into his own team's favor. They had two formations. One was quarterback under hiker, where the Quarterback would hand the ball to the runner. In the second formation, the ball would be hiked through the Quarterback's legs to the Fullback, who would then run or hand the ball left or right. Bob thought if he would fumble the wet ball, Edmore might recover it. When the ball was run to the right, Bob moved to the left. The arrogant, cocky opponent middle linebacker followed Bob away from the play. He barely made a tackle all night because he was following Bob till the end of the first half. The score at the end of the first half of the match was Shepherd: 19 and Edmore: 0. Everyone rushed to the locker room for the half-time break. They were wet, cold, and miserable.

When they returned to the field, the wet snow had covered the ground, and the winds were still howling. They could see only 30 or 40 people in the stands. Bob tried to look for the opposing team and especially that arrogant middle linebacker.

Edmore Game played in a blizzard with Bob as quarterback for Shepherd. Shepherd won 19 to 0. Visiting team left at half-time

"Their bus is gone!" A guy in the field told them. Bob was quite surprised by this foolish act from the Edmore Team.

Coach Nelson also checked with the referees, and they also told him that Edmore football team had gone back home.

"Wohoooooo!" The entire Shepherd Team cheered. They immediately rushed to the locker room to get out of their wet uniforms and into warm, dry clothes. They

finished the season six and two. The way Edmore team backed off clearly showed that as a quarterback, Bob was undefeated.
The season ended 6-2

In the spring, Bob also played on the Varsity Baseball team as a utility player outfield and infield. Bob was less than mediocre at Batting. He would always try to get the pitcher to walk him. However, he got a Varsity Letter as a sophomore and substitute player. Bob was still living with Crowleys because of sports, school, summer jobs, and no room in the trailer.

Bob and Carl and had become very good friends. Carl was a Varsity basketball player. Bob and Carl's mother Dorothy Crowley would go to watch Carl play as a Left Handed Point Guard. Mrs. Crowley was always the loudest fan in the crowd cheering for Carl's team. Bob would miss his mother so much when he would see Dorothy being happy for her son.

Shepherd school celebrated Junior Prom. It was an amazing evening with lots of fun, food and dance. Caroline looked like an Egyptian queen in her red formal gown. Bob could not take his eyes off her. It was the first time when Bob and Caroline performed together. After Mr. Duncan's death, Junior Prom was the day when Bob was truly happy. His love for Caroline was getting stronger. He could feel the same feelings in her eyes also. Life was getting back on the track. In the senior year, Bob was elected as Senior Class President living full time with the Crowleys. The new Football season was about to start.

The Shepherds football team was comparatively a small one and had many new players. The Mid-Michigan B Conference was loaded with talent. Destiny again favored Bob. Shepherd football team was scheduled to play with two B size schools rated in the top five of the state. Shepherd was a C size school which is categorically smaller than B size. Coach Nelson once again called out Bob.

"Bob! You know, getting selected to play with Mid-Michigan Conference teams is itself an achievement. I want you to play on offense and defense to help the team because we are small and have very little depth." Said the coach.

"Coach! I am ready to help in any way I can." Bob answered in an enthusiastic tone.

"Alright. You know everything about playing on defense. Now I want you to play the offensive left guard alignment." Coach instructed Bob.

Bob weighed about 150 lbs during those days. He had to learn line blocking and angles of attack. Coach Nelson coached Bob how to take advantage of anything to stop the defensive lineman.

Bob continued playing on defense for the sake of his coach and team. They lost their first game fourteen to seven. The second game of the season Shepherd played Rogers high school rated # 5 in the state for class B. The members of the opposing team were rude and immodest. They would trash talk and say negative comments about Shepherd's girls.

They tried to be as forceful and disrespectful as they could. Everyone in Bob's team began to hate their opponents as much as Bob did. The defensive lineman tackle across from him outweighed Bob by 50 to 60 pounds. These actions made Bob lose his temper. But he recalled Coach Nelson's instructions to take advantage of every move of the opponent. This thought made Bob quicker and stronger.

He constantly attacked the opponent's team. Consequently, Shepherd's team got ahead thirteen to seven in the fourth quarter.

"Come on guys, let's get it in their backfield," the opponent defensive lineman yelled at his team members.

"Shut the fuck up! You haven't gotten in our backfield all night!" Bob threw a jaw-breaking response.

The defensive lineman didn't say a single word after Bob's response. Bob continued to manhandle him with five seconds on the clock. They scored on a desperation pass in the end zone that Shepherd intercepted, but the Rogers player grabbed the ball, and the official gave the touchdown to them. Score tied thirteen to thirteen. The opposing team could still win by kicking the extra point.

We all rushed the attempt. When the opposing team hiked the ball to the holder for the extra point kick. There were five guys on the ball including Bob. They successfully blocked the attempt which resulted in no extra point for Rogers. Tie game 13-13. After that game, Bob realized they could play with anyone. Shepherd became winners and a united team that night. When Bob took his Jersey off after the game, he had muscle cramps in his biceps because of hitting the opponent so hard. Shepherds next four games were conference games that they won by 20 to 30 points each. No one scored any points on them in those four games. Their final conference game was against Chesaning High School. Their record was three wins and one tie. Shepherd's record in the conference was four wins and no losses or ties.

Shepherd and Chesaning got into the field with the zeal and dedication to win. The game began. One of the players on the Chesaning team had been severely injured in a farm accident. They wanted to dedicate the game to the injured player. Their passion to dedicate the game was probably so strong that they won thirty-two to seven. This was an unexpected defeat for Bob. He cried the whole second half. It was indeed a distressing moment for the entire team. Some of the players seemed to give up.

The back to back victories had made them addicted to winning. This was the reason they felt hopeless when they were defeated this time. Bob, however, was the one who had always moved ahead no matter what. He encouraged his team members to try once again for the victory in the next game. Their last game of the season was against Traverse City, St Francis High School.

This was a private school, and they recruited and gave scholarships to good athletes. They were rated number two in B size schools in this state. Shepherd played at their field and stayed overnight in small groups at players' homes. They were the best football team Bob had ever played against over the year. In the first play, Shepherd was on offense. They hiked the ball to Dave Dunham, the quarterback who broke his leg last year.

The defensive tackle approached Bob and knocked Bob on his ass. Thankfully, the play went to the right. Since Bob was the left guard, it saved him this time. In the next play, the same thing happened with Bob. The defensive tackle again aligned across from Bob and knocked him on his ass. It was a decisive moment for Bob. He could step aside and let the defensive tackle destroy Dave from the blindside. But that would make Bob live like a coward for the rest of his life. The other thing he could do was to try his best to stop this excellent player all night.

This was the last organized football game Bob would ever play. So he decided to step up and be a better player than he ever had been.

Go ahead and quit, if you can't see it through.

But don't come crying to me, when quitting is all you do.

Those who start to quit when things start getting tough.

Start to see quitting as a way to get out of stuff.

They never stick things through, and can't complete a thing.

Is this the type of person you see yourself being?

Quitters never win, no matter what you've heard.

Have you ever heard a quitter that is picked to be referred?

Of course, that would be silly, why would someone refer?

Someone who can't even accomplish, they are their own saboteurs.

Next time you want to quit, think who you want to be.

Quitters never win, I want more than this for thee.

I want to see success, surround you every day.

I want you to be happy, and want to scream hooray!

I want you in a job that makes your world so good.

I want the work you do, feel just like childhood.

But most of all I want, to see you see things through.

But not because you should, because you really want too.

And I realize you may be scared that you can't see it through.

But, I'm here to tell you; you can do anything you put your mind to.

-Julie Herbert

The game was very physical. On both sides, key players were out with injuries. The opponents were ahead thirteen to twelve with three to four minutes in the game. Shepherd's two best linebackers were out hurt. This was a crucial time for the entire team.

Coach Nelson was extremely worried, he said, *"Can Anyone play the middle linebacker, Come on boys, we don't have enough time."* Since Bob was playing left cornerback. He couldn't be the middle linebacker. At this climacteric moment, Bob's dearest friend Carl Crowley volunteered. Though he had never played defense in his life, he was there to help his friend as always.

Bob instructed him, *"Stand in the middle of the field behind the line with each foot shoulder-width apart. If they run up the middle, wrap your arms around his butt and your shoulder into his stomach and lift."* It was a beautiful sight to see; the Ball Carrier, who at least 50 lbs heavier than Carl, came up the middle. Carl wrapped his arms, lifted and carried the Ball Carrier back 10 yards. The Ball Carrier was kicking his feet helplessly as Carl carried him back. Bob yelled as loud as he could

"We are going to win this game!"

Shepherd finally got the ball with less than two minutes in the game. The score was Thirteen to Twelve Shepherd behind. Dave Dunham was the holder for the field goal attempt. Shepherd faked the kick. Dave threw a touchdown pass and WOW! Shepherd was ahead eighteen to thirteen. This was the final score. Bob's decision to stay in front of the defensive tackle allowed Dave Dunham to score all three touchdowns that night. Dave intercepted a pass for a touchdown, ran a quarterback sneak for a touchdown, at Bob's suggestion, and threw the touchdown pass off the fake field goal. Bob was immensely proud that he hadn't given up. After the game, the parents and the football players invited Shepherds team to a party at a huge beautiful house. Everyone had a great time, and they were a wonderful host, even though they had lost the game. Everyone at the party discussed how exciting and hard the game was.

"What position do you play on offense?" A large muscular player came close to Bob and asked.

"Left guard." Answered Bob.

"I played defensive tackle against you," the guy told Bob.

"You kicked my ass all night long as I remember the first two plays of the game" Bob hadn't forgotten that pain yet

"You are the best guard I have ever played against" the guy gave Bob the greatest compliment. *"You never gave up. The other players I have played against always give up in such situations."*

"Dave is my friend, and I knew he would get hurt if I did not protect his back." It was one of the best days of Bob's life.

The Football season ended 5-2-1. It was not bad for a team that was expected to lose the vast majority of its games.

Bob made the second-team all-conference guard in his senior year. Defensive awards were not been given in those days, but Bob felt he had been the best defensive cornerback in the conference. There were zero pass completions in two years.

Chapter 5
College Life

When things go wrong, as they sometimes will,

When the road you're trudging seems all uphill,

When the funds are low, and the debts are high,

And you want to smile, but you have to sigh,

When care is pressing you down a bit –

Rest if you must, but don't you quit.

Life is queer with its twists and turns.

As every one of us sometimes learns.

And many a fellow turns about

When he might have won had he stuck it out.

Don't give up though the pace seems slow –

You may succeed with another blow.

Often the goal is nearer than it seems to a faint and faltering man;

Often the struggler has given up

When he might have captured the victor's cup;

And he learned too late when the night came down,

How close he was to the golden crown.

Success is failure turned inside out –

The silver tint of the clouds of doubt,

And when you never can tell how close you are,
It may be near when it seems afar;
So stick to the fight when you're hardest hit –
It's when things seem worst; you must not quit.

-Edgar Albert Guest

The amazing victory in the senior year football season had enhanced Bob's self-confidence. He had been extremely content by all the praises and appreciation he had received from the people. But life had planned many more struggles for him.

During the spring of the senior year, Caroline asked Bob if he had liked her pink prom dress. Bob gave some negative comments which Caroline found offensive. She stopped dating Bob and decided to go to the senior prom with Dave Dunham.

Bob became extremely upset as it was not a fair reason to break up. He didn't attend the senior prom because it would be painful for him to see Caroline and Dave dancing with each other. It was a warm Wednesday afternoon in the spring. Bob and four of his friends had been having their lunch at school during the break.

All of a sudden, one of Bob's friends said, *"I need to go to Ithaca to pick up a part for my car at my uncle's house. Let's go together."*

"But we are not allowed to go in the middle of the school day." Another friend argued. However, after some discussion, we all agreed to skip school. One of the boys knew a girl student who worked in the principal's office. He requested her to approve their excuse slips the next day when they would go to the school. All the boys were really excited because it was no less than an adventure for them.

"We must get some beer too." One of the guys came up with this idea.

The driver knew someone over twenty-one years old who would buy beer for them. They were well aware that a car with five students and the beer buyer might look suspicious in our small town. So they decided to wait at the country road while the driver and the beer buyer would go into the town. Meanwhile, the boys had been standing at the country road, a car passed by them. The superintendent of schools had been driving that car. He knew each of the boys by their name.

He stared at them for a few minutes and drove off. All the boys were quite nervous as they could sense a huge problem coming their way. After about thirty minutes, the driver came to pick them, leaving the beer buyer in town. It was a troublesome situation for all of them. They sat together and made some plans for the next day while drinking beer.

They didn't want the girls in the principal's office to get in trouble. So they just went to the school the next day leaving everything to their fate. They were all called out of their first class and sent to the principal's office. The principal Mr. Bates was sitting at his desk. He was a small man with a huge IQ. He looked up at them, standing in front of his desk and very quietly asked.

"Why are you here?"

One of the boys answered, *"You know why we are here."*

He looked up at them from his chair and said, *"No. You tell me why the five of you are here."*

One of Bob's friends narrated the entire story. Mr. Bates listened to him and calmly said, *"All of you are out of school and may return Monday morning. You will receive zero grade for any test you miss on Thursday and Friday."*

"You can leave my office but don't go to any classes." He added.

Bob and all of his friends got in Carl Crowley's car and went to Carl's house. They played poker until school almost was dismissed, then Carl took everyone back to the school so they could ride the bus home. They repeated the same thing the next day.

When they returned to the school on Monday, their wonderful teachers had forgotten the threat of giving them zero grades for those two days. Bob scored the best grades in his final exams of high school. Bob received 4 A's and 1 B.

****

Those were the last days of his senior year in high school. One fine day, Coach Nelson had been teaching them accounting. Bob had been busy making notes of the lecture. Coach Nelson came close to Bob's desk and asked him,

"Bob! What do you intend to do after graduating high school?"

"I will try to find a good job. Maybe one at a local chemical factory." As Bob had already decided about his future, he answered at once.

"C'mon, Bob! You are too smart for doing such a mediocre job. You must go to college to continue your studies." Coach Nelson advised him.

"Coach! Do you have any insight into my life and its sufferings? I am basically homeless, living with Crowley's without any financial support from my family." Bob didn't like Coach's idea; he replied angrily.

"That's BULLSHIT! If I could go to college even after having a difficult life, why can't you?" Coach Nelson Roared.

"I know it is difficult for you to work for your living expenses, but it can be done along with the studies." Coach further added.

"Really? Show me how." Bob was still not convinced.

After about a week, Coach gave him a prospectus from Ferris State College. It explained everything, including the application process, tuition fees, curriculum, and Prerequisites. Bob wanted to pursue further education in accounting, but according to the Ferris curriculum, he was overqualified to choose his major in accounting.

He had studied chemistry, physics, geometry, trigonometry, and biology during his high school and had passed all the subjects with good grades. Ferris offered a degree in pharmacy which matched Bob's high school curriculum. He decided to give it a shot and asked Coach Nelson about it. Though Coach had not enough knowledge about pharmacy, he set up a meeting with a local pharmacist named Stu. They went to meet Stu and Bob shared his concerns with him. He said,

"You will always have a job as soon as you have a degree in pharmacy."

It sounded quite interesting to Bob. He suddenly recalled those days when his father had lost his job in Detroit as a middle-aged adult with an eighth-grade education. They had to survive on welfare.

"But a pharmacist can never get rich." Stu further added.

At that time, getting rich was not Bob's goal. He wanted to pursue his career in a field which would assure him job security.

"If I get enrolled in Pharmacy and in case I find it difficult to continue, will it be possible to switch my major to accounting?" Bob was puzzled as he had never thought about studying pharmacy in college.

"Yes. Students can change their majors anytime." Stu confirmed, and Coach Nelson seconded him. Bob had been quite satisfied after meeting Stu; therefore, he began the application process.

His mother contributed the initial application fee. His teachers and other elderly people he knew gave him letters of recommendation which were mandatory as a part of the application process. Finally, Bob's admission was approved by the Ferris College which had been located at Big Rapids, Michigan sixty miles away from Shepherd High School. But he had no money to fund his day to day expenses.

It was crucial for him to find a job as early as possible. After getting admission at Ferris College, Bob requested his mother to ask one of his uncles, Mr. John Lee, to help him get a job at the Ford foundry in Cleveland, Ohio. Uncle John was an executive at the plant, and he had his own parking space with his name on it. Uncle John hired him and allowed Bob to live at his home free of cost in the summer to save some money for his college.

Bob began working in the foundry as a janitor. He would clean restrooms. Workers poured hot and dirty molten steel for engine blocks all day long. When Bob returned to Shepherd shortly before the college had started, he had saved one thousand dollars.

After returning to Shepherd, Bob contacted Caroline once again to see if their mutual attraction was still alive. Bob was extremely glad when Caroline accepted his request for a date. The romance was rekindled, and soon, they decided to spend the rest of their lives together. During his freshman year, Bob stayed in the Dormitory with his roommate Jack Karner. Caroline attended a twelve-month Medical Technology School in Elkhart, Indiana.

Bob would visit Caroline in Indiana whenever it would be possible for him. Finally, Bob completed his freshman year with a 3.2 GPA. During the freshman year, Bob had joined the Marine Corps officer training program which entailed six weeks of basic training in the summer between his freshman and sophomore year. It didn't prove to be a good decision because Bob had no income for that summer. However, he began working at a gas station. Meanwhile, Caroline had finished the Lab School and started working in a hospital at Mount Pleasant. She also helped Bob financially whenever he needed it.

Bob got a student loan for two hundred and fifty dollars and also worked in the cafeteria at the college for 78 cents an hour. The money did not help much because of classes and short working hours. The only benefit of working in the cafeteria was the ability to take food back to his dormitory room. Sports practice became impossible for Bob when he was advanced to courses such as organic chemistry, Physics, Botany, Pharmacology, and Microbiology. In the advanced courses, it was vital to use a slide ruler for calculations.

Bob had never used a Slide Rule for calculations in his life, which was a precursor to a pocket calculator. It became quite difficult for him to understand the calculations. His fellow students would mock Bob for his clothing, his farm background with the Crowley's and his Poor English. Bob noticed that he couldn't do well on exams from professors that had been teaching at the college for a long period of time, whereas the pharmacy fraternity students would do really well in these tests.

Bob would score good grades in the tests by the new professors. It seemed quite shady to him, and he began investigating this issue. He discovered that each fraternity kept a file of old tests by professors and they would use them as study guides for their fraternity members. Bob had been friends with two or three fraternity members who verified his suspicions.

Once a guy named Rick Crandall approached Bob. He wanted to study with Bob for a new professor's exams. Bob put on a condition. He said

"Get me the old test for organic chemistry and Physics, and we can study together for the new professor's exam."

Rick Crandall denied the fraternities had copies of old tests, and Bob said

"Sorry, Rick! Then we cannot study together."

However, Rick came back to Bob shortly and said

"I have an old test. Can we study together for the new professor?"

"Yes. For sure." Bob answered.

From that time, Rick and Bob passed all their courses and became good friends.

Bob and Caroline decided to get married on April 8, 1961.

From Left to Right

Verna Whalen (Caroline's Mom), Caroline, Bob, Emma (Bob's Mom)

Wedding Day
4/8/1961

They had a plan that Caroline would continue working at the hospital in Mount Pleasant and Bob would work with Stu, the pharmacist at Shepherd during the summers and weekends. Stu had offered him $1.25 an hour. Bob and Caroline would live in Big Rapids during the week. Caroline would commute forty miles to Mt. Pleasant hospital, and Bob would work weekends at the pharmacy in Shepherd. In June 1961, Caroline became pregnant.

She lost her job at the hospital in Mount Pleasant because the hospital felt it was not safe for a pregnant woman to drive forty miles each way on country roads in Michigan winters. To supplement this income, Caroline got a job of babysitting three children under three years old in cloth diapers for twenty-five dollars a week.

Caroline would experience morning sickness every day, but she had to rinse out the cloth diapers of those three kids. It was the toughest time of her life, but she did it until Colleen was born on March 20th, 1962. Student loans had been almost impossible to get. Bob and Caroline could borrow three hundred and fifty dollars only, which put them in an impossible situation. Bob had to take extra classes to catch up for his short schedule during his sophomore year. He had already dropped a few electives in his sophomore year. Bob now enrolled in twenty-one hours against the advice of the advisor. The adviser thought it was impossible to take twenty-one hours with labs in the pharmacy curriculum.

However, Bob passed the twenty-one hours and caught up to graduate on schedule. In his third year after

Colleen had been born, Caroline had to take care of their baby. So her income of twenty-five dollars a week was gone, and they had been left Bob's paycheck of Twelve dollars and fifty cents a week.

Bob met Marine Corp recruiters at the college and was shocked to learn the Marines were NOT allowed to sign up pharmacy students. After discussing the situation, Bob decided to follow the suggestion of the recruiters and transfer to the Marine Reserve, which entailed one weekend meeting, each month during his senior year and thirty days active duty each year until his six-year obligation was complete. Bob received an honorable discharge Feb. 1966.

Bob's mother had divorced Louie a few months before bob's and Caroline's marriage. She had a nervous breakdown out of the trauma. After she had sunk deeper into depression, she finally admitted herself into Traverse, the city mental hospital for a minimum of ninety days at the strong suggestion of Dorothy Crowley. Upon discharge, Emma moved in with Bob and Caroline because she had worn out her welcome at the Crowley's household. Her medications cost twelve dollars and fifty cents a month. Bob had to pay for it from his limited income.

Bob and Caroline had been going through a huge financial crisis. Bob met the assistant dean of the pharmacy with plans to drop out of college. The Assistant Dean said,

"Bob! There are only six weeks left until school is out for the summer."

Bob explained the severity of this situation to the assistant dean. He offered Bob the aid of one hundred dollars. It would truly be a great help for Bob. He gratefully accepted the aid.

After a few months, Bob's mother felt mentally stable. She got a job taking care of an elderly lady for a small amount of money. So, Emma moved out from living with Bob and Caroline. Caroline always checked with the local hospital to keep her resume active. Sometimes, she got part-time employment at the hospital.

In their junior year, she got a call from the hospital, asking her to work full-time. Starting, June 1st, 1962, she took the job. She was the only lab technician and was on call 24 hours a day, seven days a week. Plus, she had regular work shifts.

At this time, Bob decided to take a six-hour pharmacology course with two, three-hour labs in the summer. The summer was enjoyable because it was the only class that he took. And it reduced Bob's academic load his senior year. Bob organized an intramural softball team that did very well. He had a great summer. Bob played third base and batted almost 700 with the larger and slower ball.

Times were really good. They had a small apartment and the lady they rented from loved Colleen, so Bob had plenty of free time. Bob was finally enjoying college life. In October of Bob’s senior year, Caroline got pregnant. They calculated that the baby would be born in June. So, Caroline could keep working for the rest of the year. Carin was born on June 1st, 1963, and Bob graduated on June 9th, 1963.

Bob graduating College

After graduation, Bob and Caroline moved to Gladwin, Michigan for two years and Bob worked in a local drugstore. Those were the happiest days for the Duncan family. Bob and Caroline felt that their hard work had paid off. Life had finally fallen on the right track.

Chapter 6
Trial

Every scar has a story.
What will mine tell?
What will come of this?
When I'm better when I'm well?
I want my scar to tell
Of how I've overcome,
Of how I made it through,
Of where I have come from.
I want my scar to whisper
About the pain I faced,
About this very hard time,
About the marathon, I raced.
But mostly I want my scar
To speak of something greater
I want it to shout
About my living Creator.
Let my scar be evidence
That there is a loving Lord,
Who fought my scary battles
And on whose wings I soared.

Let my scar proclaim
That all things work for good,
That by myself I couldn't
But with my God, I could.
Let them take a look.
Let them peek and see.
My scar shows God is great.
It points to Him, not me.

-Kristina M. DeCarlo

Caroline received the news of another pregnancy in the middle of 1964. Bob was delighted as they had always dreamed of having three children. Caroline gave birth to Mike on April 26, 1965. Shortly after Mike's birth, Bob and Caroline moved back to their hometown, Shepherd, along with their three children. Bob began working at a pharmacy called Post pharmacy situated in Mount Pleasant. They lived a simple and peaceful life.

One sunny morning, Caroline was preparing a surprise breakfast in the kitchen. No one was allowed to enter the kitchen. Bob and the two elder kids were waiting at the breakfast table with their stomachs churning with both hunger and anticipation. Mike was crawling on the floor.

"Caroline! Why is your surprise taking forever?" Bob was starving. He looked at Colleen and Carin, who were busy discussing their favorite cartoon show. Bob grabbed the morning newspaper. He glanced over the first page. It was full of bland news. He was about to turn the page when he saw something that shook him up. It was the headline of an article which read

"Graham, the murderer of Gene Duncan, declared sane. Trial set on April 30th, 1966."

The man who had killed his father on September 2, 1956, was going on trial for murder and kidnapping. This news awakened all of the bad memories for Bob. It had taken him years to build a life for himself. Now after nine and a half years, this news reopened his old wounds. It seemed everything had happened only yesterday.

"Here's the surprise!" Caroline entered the living area holding the breakfast tray in her hands. Bob looked at her with a hollow smile. His hunger had vanished.

****

Two weeks had passed after this shocking news. Bob received a call from Edward Duran, the prosecuting attorney of Mr. Duncan's case.

"Bob! You must've read the news about the declaration of Graham's sanity." Duran said.

"Yes, Mr. Duran. I did. We haven't been able to sleep well ever since." Bob replied in a heavy voice.

"I understand your situation. I need to interview Mrs. Emma Duncan and you concerning the events of that terrible day." Duran explained.

Bob felt his heart twist. *"Mr. Duran! My mother took years to recover from the incident that threw her in the depths of depression and months in a mental hospital. I don't want her to endure this pain once again."*

"I understand, but don't you want the murderer of your father to pay the price for what he's done to you and your family?" Duran asked.

"I do. Who else would want that more than me? I just don't want my mother to get hurt anymore." Bob replied in a miserable voice.

"It will not hurt your mother. It will bring her peace. Last week, on April 22nd, Graham had a hearing with four renowned psychiatrists. He was found sane for trial. This is God's way of justice." Duran answered firmly.

"I want you and your mother to visit me at my office this Thursday. I want to prepare you both for the coming trial." Duran added.

"Umm... Alright. I'll be there with my mother." Bob heaved a deep sigh.

****

Bob and Emma visited Duran's office on Thursday afternoon. Duran asked them detailed questions about the ordeal. Emma kept sobbing throughout the interview. She missed her husband to the core. Bob put his arms around his mother to comfort her. It was extremely painful for the two to recall the events that had turned their world upside down.

"Mr. Duran! I want you to convict this Graham bastard! He killed my father for no reason. He destroyed our family. He deserves a life sentence!" Bob's face distorted with rage.

"Relax, Bob. Calm down. Conviction is out of my hands. It is the judge's call. Just stay confident in the courtroom. Graham's defense attorney will try his best to mold the case in their favor." Duran explained.

"You know Mr. Duran... I will always regret that I couldn't tell my father how much I loved him. I was a typical teenager who always had his own things to do. I never appreciated him for everything he did for us. I always thought that I would admire my father sometime in future. I had no idea life would never give me this chance. That day when my father was lying on the floor before me, in the pool of his blood, I wanted to hug him. I wanted to tell him that I couldn't live without him..." Bob burst out into tears. He bawled like a child. Emma patted him on the back. She was crying just as much as he was.

Bob pulled out his handkerchief from his pocket and blew his nose into it. *"Today, I am happily married. I have three children. I love my family immensely. When my wife and children express their love and affection to me, I feel blessed. I have now understood how important it is to tell someone that you love them. You never know what will happen the very next moment. Life seldom gives you a second chance."* Bob continued in a raspy voice.

Duran got up from his chair and came close to Bob. He patted his shoulders and said, *"Bob! We can't change what has happened. Be brave. We have to bring the killer of your father to justice."*

Bob nodded.

****

It was July 13th, 1966. The day of the trial had finally arrived. Graham was represented by two lawyers who were from Grosse Pointe Michigan, an old affluent area adjacent to Detroit. They had requested a non-jury trial. They wanted to take the emotional aspect of the jury out of the decision.

A non-jury or bench trial takes place in front of a judge only. There is no jury involved. The judge is both the finder of fact and ruler on matters of law and procedure. It depicts that the judge decides the credibility of the evidence presented at the trial. A non-jury trial can be beneficial when people want a speedy resolution to a legal matter. It usually takes less time than jury trials because the attorneys do not need to go through the jury selection and instruction process. Bench trials are slightly less formal than jury trials. They are useful in particularly complex cases that a jury may not be able to understand[1].

Bob and Emma reached the courtroom at 8:40 AM.

The trial began at 9:00 AM. Mrs. Duncan was called first to the witness box. She was asked to testify. She said,

"It was the morning of September 2, 1956. We were all asleep. I woke up to the pounding on our door. I glanced over at the table clock. It was 6:30 AM. I got up and went to the door to see who it was, so I could tell them we won't be open until 9:00 AM. There was a tall man standing at the door. It was Graham.

I told him that the store was closed and it would open at 9:00 AM. I was about to turn around when he said that

---

[1]Rome McGuigan, P.C. Attorney At law. (2019). What is the difference between a bench trial and a jury trial? Website. Retrieved from: https://www.rms-law.com/Articles/What-is-the-Difference-Between-a-Bench-Trial-and-a-Jury-Trial.shtml

he was out of gas and he needed it urgently. He pleaded me to open the store. I felt sorry for the poor man and agreed to help him. I went inside, put on my housecoat. I turned ON the gas pumps. Then I went outside to pump gas for his car…." Emma stopped for a few seconds to breathe.

"As soon as I was done filling up the gas in his car, he pulled a gun on me. He told me to go with him or else he would shoot me. It was quite a shock for me. I was very scared. I tried to resist, but he threatened that he would kill everybody inside my home if I didn't do everything he said. I found no option other than going with him. He forced me into his car and drove to the town of Midland. After driving a few miles down the road, he suddenly took a U-turn and headed back to the store. He had beaten up his girlfriend at Mount Pleasant. He was afraid that she might have given his car description to the police. He decided to return to the store and get my husband's car…" Emma's mouth had turned so dry that it was hard for her to speak. She breathed for a few seconds, then continued again.

"When we entered our house, Mr. Duncan had been awake and dressed. When he saw an unknown man following me inside, he shouted and asked what the matter was. Before I could say anything, Graham shot him in his arm and leg. He immediately fell to the floor, bleeding profusely. I was dumbfounded on the sight of so much blood. I wanted to save my husband, but it felt as if my feet were stuck to the floor. Graham then stood over him and shot him twice in the chest."

Emma stopped as the scene of that horrible shooting flashed in front of her. It was as if she had stepped back into that day and had no control over changing anything. All she could do was live everything all over again. She was helpless. She continued after a minute, gaining control over herself.

"He pulled his gun on me and asked me to give him Mr. Duncan's car keys. I knew Bob was inside. If I hadn't handed him the keys, he would have killed my son too. Graham then forced me into Mr. Duncan's Buick and drove the car towards Midland. A few miles ahead, we were stopped at a police roadblock and Graham was arrested." Mrs. Duncan broke into tears. Her sobbing

echoed around the entire courtroom. After a few minutes, Emma was asked to take a seat again, and Bob was called to the stand. He began testifying as to the events of that day flashed by his eyes.

"It was about 7:30 AM... I heard the shots and thought that the TV was ON. I didn't pay much attention and got up to get dressed. When I entered the living room, I was dazed to see my father lying on the floor, drenched in blood...I rushed towards him and asked him what had happened. Even after being shot in the chest, he was quite calm. He didn't want me to panic. He told me that an unknown man had shot him and taken my mother with him. I was furious when I heard that. I wanted to kill that bastard...I asked my dad about his shotgun and shells. He told me that he had kept them in the closet.

He then asked me to call the police and our family friends - Crowleys. I rushed to the store to phone both of them. I looked out of the store window to see if the shooter was still there, but I couldn't find anyone. After calling the Midland police and the Crowleys, I returned to the living room. I took out the shotgun from the closet, loaded it and sat on the couch with the shotgun pointed at the front door. I wanted to destroy the scoundrel who had hurt my parents. After about twenty minutes, the police came along with the ambulance. The ambulance took my father to the hospital. I talked to the police briefly about the incident. After a few minutes, Bert Crowley arrived at our place. We all went to the hospital." Bob had managed to keep his emotions under control while he testified. He didn't want to miss out on any details.

"You may go now." The defense attorney said as Bob finished his statement.

"Your honor! Now I want to call one of the renowned psychiatrists in the witness box who interviewed Graham in jail." The defense attorney asked the judge. The judge nodded.

The psychiatrist testified,

"I interviewed Graham in jail. He showed all the signs of a mentally unbalanced person who didn't know the difference between right and wrong."

"So you mean to say a mentally unbalanced person can do anything without being aware of the consequences." The defense attorney said.

"Objection your honor! The defense attorney is trying to justify the crime." Edward Duran raised the objection.

"Objection sustained." The judge said.

"Thank you, your honor! I want to call one of the police officers in the witness box, who was there at the roadblock?" Said Duran. The judge nodded.

When the police officer came into the witness box, Duran asked,

"What did you analyze about Graham's mental status by his behavior on September 2, 1956?"

"Objection your honor! *The prosecution attorney cannot ask such questions. The police officer is not a licensed psychiatrist to evaluate Graham's mental status."* The defense attorney raised the objection.

"Objection sustained." The judge agreed with the objection.

Duran shrugged his shoulders in a defeated manner. He then decided to ask some general questions to the police officer.

"Roadblock consisted of police cars and police officers in uniform. Is that correct?" Duran asked, lacing his fingers together.

"Yes." The police officer answered.

"Umm... When Graham approached the roadblock. Did he slow down or speed up?" Duran asked another question.

"He slowed down and stopped the car as instructed." The police officer replied, confidently.

"When you stopped him, what did he say?" Duran asked in a thoughtful manner.

"He said that he had just killed a guy back there. I was quite astounded on this answer. I interrogated him about the car. He told me that it was not his car. The car belonged to the man he had just killed. He even told me that he had taken this car forcefully from Mrs. Duncan. Meanwhile, I was questioning Graham, Mrs. Duncan got out of the car and told us that this man had killed her

husband and forced her to come with him in Mr. Duncan's car. She revealed that she had to go with him or else he would have killed her too." the police officer gave complete details.

"Right... So how was Mrs. Duncan's condition at that time?" Duran put forward another question.

"She was hysterical. She was crying hard and screaming." The police officer briefed.

"Thank you for the details, gentleman. You may go now." Duran thanked the police officer and slowly turned around.

"Your honor! Graham not only killed an innocent man, but he also tried to kidnap Mrs. Duncan. He should be charged with murder and kidnapping." Duran presented his stance.

"Your honor. The prosecution attorney has forgotten that according to the evaluation of four psychiatrists, Graham was insane when he killed Mr. Duncan. He was mentally unbalanced even when he was evaluated in jail. How can a mentally unstable man be charged with these

felonies?" The defense attorney stressed on Graham's insanity.

There was pin-drop silence in the courtroom. A few minutes passed, the prosecution attorney got up. He harrumphed and said.

"Your honor! According to the facts presented in the court, I am convinced that Mr. Graham may have been insane when he killed Mr. Duncan and in the jail after the murder, not knowing the difference between right and wrong. However, according to the roadblock police officer, he certainly knew the difference between right and wrong, and when he approached the roadblock. He slowed down his car.

A person cannot be sane and insane at the same time. It sounds quite odd that he kidnapped Mrs. Duncan out of his poor mental state, but at the same time, he was quite sane to follow the highway rules. Insanity is not a defense for kidnapping when he obeys the law. So here, I am dropping the murder charge; however, I will retain the kidnapping charge." Duran presented his viewpoint.

"Objection your honor." The defense attorney pushed back his chair and rose.

"Objection overruled." The judge disagreed to the objection. The defense slumped back in his chair in a defeated manner.

"The final verdict will be given on July 19th, 1966, at 1:00 PM sharp. The court is adjourned for the day." the hearing was brought to an end.

****

On July 19th, Bob and Emma couldn't gather enough courage to go to the court for the verdict. If Graham was found innocent in the kidnapping charge because of his insanity, it would be extremely devastating for them. However, Bob anxiously waited for Duran's call to know about the judge's verdict. Finally, Duran called him at about 2:00 PM.

"There is good news for you, Bob." Duran seemed quite delighted.

"Graham had been found guilty of kidnapping. He is sentenced for seventeen years." Duran broke the good news to him. Bob couldn't believe his ears. They had

waited for this day for years. Finally, God brought his fathers killer to justice. He heaved a sigh of relief.

"Thanks a lot, Mr. Duran. It couldn't have been possible without your efforts. We were at the verge of losing this case. I can't thank you enough for helping me get justice for my father. This was the only way to tell my dad how much I love him." Bob was overwhelmed. Tears rolled down his eyes.

"God never does injustice to innocents. Stay blessed Bob," said Duran. He hung up the phone. His face expanded into a beaming grin. He knew he had done a good job.

****

In the afternoon, Duran was on his way home. A strange feeling had occupied his mind. He didn't understand what it was. Suddenly he saw a store with a payphone. He stopped for a while and thought about something.

He headed towards the store and dropped a quarter into the slot of the payphone. He dialed a number, but no one picked up the call. He dialed again. It was picked up after five rings.

"Hello, Dad! Duran here." He said.

"Duran? Is everything fine son? You never call at this time." His father was concerned about him.

"Yeah, Dad! I just wanted to say that...." He breathed for a few seconds.

"I wanted to say that I Love You." Duran poured his heart out.

Graham's case had made him realize that *if we love someone, we should always tell them.*

God gave each of us a special family
That we can call our own.
A family that loves us for who we are
So we would never feel alone.
They may not like everything we do
Or everything we say,
But the beautiful thing about "family"
Is that they love us anyway.
Sometimes we feel rejected
By people who do not care,
But our hearts are warmed when remembering
That our family is always there!

So hug them a little more often,
For sometimes we hurt the ones we love.
And tell them how much you love them,
For they were sent to you from above.
-Josephine Zavala-Florez

Bob & Caroline with grandchildren
Left – Cole
Right – Finn
Lights of our life

Bob & Caroline after approx. 40 years of marriage